Rosie

Written by Sarah Prince
Illustrated by Mitch Vane

sundance

My brother and I don't like our baby-sitter
She is too neat, too tidy, and too bossy.
She's just no fun!

She always makes us take a bath.
She always makes us brush our teeth.
She always makes us go to bed.
She never lets us stay up late.

3

One night, when Mom and Dad were going out, our baby-sitter couldn't come. Her sister came instead.

"Hello," she said. "I'm Rosie Moon."

Rosie Moon looked at us.
We looked at Rosie Moon.
Somehow we knew she was
different from her sister.

"What shall we do?" asked Rosie Moon.

"Let's watch TV," we said.

"I have another idea," said Rosie Moon. "Let's bake a cake instead."

We baked a cake. We put green icing
and lots of decorations on it.
It was the best cake we had ever made.

"That's delicious," my brother said.

"Let's bake something else," I said.

"I have another idea," said Rosie Moon.

"Let's paint some pictures instead,"
said Rosie Moon. "Close your eyes and
·imagine you are on a faraway planet."

"I can see strange creatures floating
above the ground," I said.

"I can see spaceships landing
on the moon," my brother said.

We' painted the most spectacular pictures.

"Let's paint another picture," said my
brother.

"I have another idea," said Rosie Moon.

"Let's have a puppet show instead."

We made puppets with arms and legs
and ears and eyes. We used string to
make the puppets move up and down.
We had the best puppet show ever.

"Let's have another puppet show," I said.

"I have another idea," said Rosie Moon.

"Let's make some music instead."

"I'll play the trumpet," said my brother.

"I'll play the drums," I said.

"I'll hum," said Rosie Moon.

We made the best music.

"Let's do it again," said my brother.

"Not now," said Rosie Moon.
"It's bedtime."

"Oh no, we can't go to bed," I said.

"We have to choose something for Show and Tell at school tomorrow," said my brother.

"What are you going to do?" asked Rosie Moon.

"We don't know!" we cried.

Then Rosie Moon had another great idea.

"Why don't you take all of the things we made tonight?" she said.

"Great idea," I said.

"Fantastic," said my brother.

15

The next day, Mom and Dad asked us
how we liked our new baby-sitter.
"We're over the moon about Rosie,"
we said.